shopping

it's the little **voices** that tell me to go **shopping**

Vimr⬚d by Lisa Swerling and Ralph Lazar

HarperCollins*Entertainment*

An Imprint of HarperCollins*Publishers*

deep, **deep** inside the brain of every woman is a small **bungalow** in which lives a little lady who is

totally obsessed with shoes

stop the world

i want
to get off
and go
shopping

ever get the feeling your credit card is laughing at you?

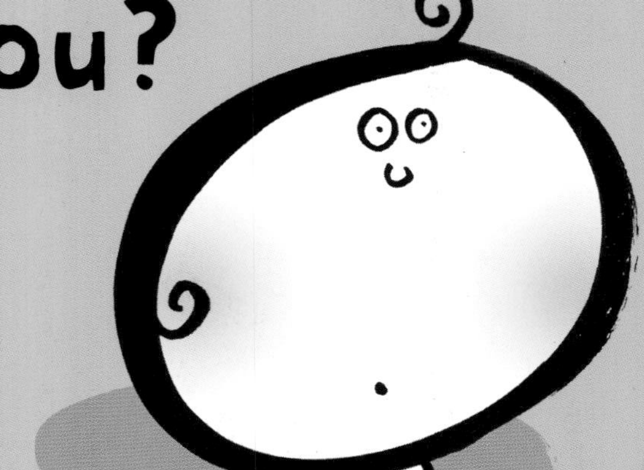

the contemporary
hunter-gatherer
is she who can
pick up men
whilst
shopping

you know the way men **shout** when they watch football?

"Oooow!!"

Resulttt! YES!! GOAL!

Aw REF!!

imagine if women shouted like that when they went shopping.

the government phoned.
it told me,
to help the economy,
i must do

more shopping.

i find it a bit weird, but
i am fully prepared
to help out.

i have a PhD in accessories

be **very careful** of the entrances to shopping malls

(one minute you'll be
innocently walking by,
the next you are
sucked in and have to
do some shopping)

it's `hard` being a woman;

which handbag?
which skirt?
which shoes?
which man?
which chocolate?

life is
fantastic

(with
plastic)

i shop

therefore

i

am

the phase of the moon suggests to me

that we should be
shopping

the great thing

about progress is that there are still more shopping malls to be built

if we really wanted to,
us women would completely
rule the world.

the thing is, do we
really want to?

no, we'd rather
go shopping.

god created woman.

he looked at her and saw that she was good.

then he created shopping, chocolate, shoes, wine and various different types of magazine.

then he sat back, burped, farted, and then god created man.

i am your handbag

and am fully prepared to hang out

under your armpits.

call that dedication
or what?

deep
inside the brain
of every woman is
another brain,
and inside that another,
and then another,
and inside that last one is a
microscopic and well-stocked
shopping mall

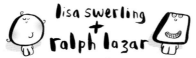

lisa swerling + ralph lazar

are two of the UK's most familiar
graphic artists. Through their company
Last Lemon they have spawned a catwalk
of popular cartoon characters, which
includes Harold's Planet, The Brainwaves,
Blessthischick and, of course, Vimrod.

Writers, artists and designers, they are
married with two children, and spend
their time between London and various
beaches on the Indian Ocean.

- -

HarperCollins*Entertainment*

An Imprint of HarperCollins*Publishers*

77–85 Fulham Palace Road, Hammersmith, London W6 8JB

www.harpercollins.co.uk

Published by HarperCollins*Entertainment* 2006

2

A catalogue record for this book is available from the British Library

ISBN-13   978 0 00 723415 8

Set in Bokka

Printed and bound in Italy by Lego SpA

other titles in the **Vimrod** collection:

drink!

wine is made to be **drunk**,
I am drunk,
therefore
am i wine?

xmas

christmas is
coming
run!

farting

my farts
hospitalise
small
children

(watch
this
space)